THE MAKING
Includes Study Companion and Journal

Vera LeRay Warner

Copyright © 2017 by Vera LeRay Warner

All rights reserved. No part of this book shall be reproduced or transmitted in any form or by any means, electronic, mechanical, magnetic, photographic including photocopying, recording or by any information storage and retrieval system, without prior written permission of the publisher. No patent liability is assumed with respect to the use of the information contained herein. Although every precaution has been taken in preparation of this book, the publisher and author assume no responsibility for errors or omissions. Neither is any liability assumed for damages resulting from the use of the information contained herein.

Unless otherwise indicated, all Scripture quotations are taken from the Amplified Bible Version of the Bible. Scripture taken from THE AMPLIFIED BIBLE, Old Testament Copyright ©1965, 1987 by the Zondervan Corporation. THE AMPLIFIED NEW TESTAMENT Copyright ©1958, 1987 by the Lockman Foundation. Used by permission."

"Scripture taken from THE MESSAGE, Copyright © by Eugene H. Peterson, 1993, 1994, 1996. Used by permission of NavPress Publishing Group."

Scripture quotations marked (NLT) are taken from the Holy Bible, New Living Translation, copyright © 1996. Used by permission of Tyndale House Publishers, Inc., Wheaton, Illinois 60108. All rights reserved.

Scripture quotations marked (NKJV) are taken from *the New King James Version*©1979, 1980, 1982, 1984 by Thomas Nelson, Inc. Used by permission.

While the author has made every effort to provide accurate Internet addresses at the time of publication, neither the author nor the publisher assumes any responsibility for errors or for changes that occur after publication.

ISBN 978-0-9989232-1-5

Published by:

In His Image Publishing
P.O. Box 291924
Columbia, SC 29229

Printed in the United States of America
Printed on Recycled Paper

DEDICATION

I dedicate this book to "A Mother to More than Her Own" Queen Sutton. At this writing, Miss Queen is more than 80 years old and her testimony is one of struggle and courage and favor and wisdom. What a wonderful light in the Kingdom of God and I love and respect you more than I can adequately express. You are truly a "Queen"!

CONTENTS

Acknowledgements	i
Preface	ii
How to Use the Study Companion and Journal	v
Introduction	vii
Chapter One. First Thing's First "I Am Responsible For My Own Choices"	1
Chapter Two. A Walking Sermon "I Am a Living Epistle"	12
Chapter Three. Epiphany of Purpose "Up-close and Personal"	22
Chapter Four. The Making of Me	35
Chapter Five. Get the Little Foxes: A Study on Integrity	52
Chapter Six. Accountability I've Fallen and I Can Get Up	65
Chapter Seven. A Minister Ain't Nothing but a Servant (A Review on Servanthood)	78
Bibliography	91
About the Author	92

ACKNOWLEDGEMENTS

I wish to thank my husband, Michael, for his unconditional love and support. Honey, so many times, you have stood in the shadows and allowed me to shine, and I am so grateful. I am a blessed woman indeed!

I offer thanks to the present board of In His Image: Women of Excellence; Lorraine, Diana, Jackie, Dana, Paula, Andrea, Gabi, Joyce, Erica, and Carol. You guys are amazing and I love you all tons!

Thank you to some of the most powerful praying women on the planet; Patricia, Samantha, Angela, Jackie T., Sharon, Marjorie, Daniela and Mona. Oh, what miraculous answers to prayer on the line. You ladies are awesome!

Thank you to Maureen Johnson and Yolanda O'Neal. It would have been a hot mess if the two of you had not come to the rescue! Your proofing skills are matchless.

Finally, but not least of all to my Lord and Savior, Jesus Christ. Father, I cannot even begin to express my gratitude for your, "Making of Me!" This work in progress is one grateful lady. Thank you, Abba!

PREFACE

My family and I were coming to the end of a four-year long tour of duty in beautiful Oahu, Hawaii. During this time, we had been extremely blessed to be a member of the Newtown Church of God. It was a thriving body of believers whereby we were graced to have been first-hand witnesses of the manifold grace of God, including miracles, signs, and wonders. The four years had been a time of tremendous spiritual growth for my family and me and it would be a time in our lives that we would never forget.

Our Women's Ministries, under the leadership of Sharon Powell, was a model ministry for lack of a better description. Our meetings were not normal by any means. It was a common occurrence for us to show up at a meeting thinking that it would be a normal time of fellowship and fun and it turned out to be oh so much more than that. God never failed to show up and show out! During our meetings, women gave their hearts to the Lord, were filled with the Holy Spirit, delivered from strongholds of the enemy, accepted calls to the ministry and were physically healed. Therefore, it was no wonder that on that afternoon during one of our annual banquets, that my Lord spoke so plainly to me to give me comfort and direction before making the next permanent change of duty station.

I cannot even remember the speaker's name that day. But, what I do remember is that at the end of her message she said, "There is someone here that the Lord wants to minister to. The Lord is saying that just like Philip the Evangelist, the Lord is taking you from a place where for the past few years you have experienced real revival. And he is taking you to a place that will seem like a desert in comparison. Nevertheless, do not be discouraged because He will use you there. He is sending you on assignment and you will minister to people of renown; doctors and lawyers and people of wealth, the elite." I sat there in my chair that afternoon as the words were coming forth and just wept and wept, as my Lord seemed to just burn the words in my heart. I sat there sobbing as his presence just washed over me in waves. For many days afterwards, I imagined how God would accomplish what he had spoken to my heart. I imagined myself in a church being introduced, walking up to the podium and giving my testimony of the goodness of my Lord. Oh, how limited I was in my imagining how the Lord would bring to pass His will.

Soon after my family and I were transferred to Fort Devens, Massachusetts, and to make a long story short, in comparison to what we had just left, it would prove to be a desert in every sense of the word! But before I go on, I must say that I would not have traded my time there for anything in the world. Those three years were a time of testing and heartache and sorrow and joy and peace. It was a time of tremendous spiritual growth. I learned many lessons there and I thank God for the fire of testing.

Very soon after arriving, I was blessed to get a job at Sundance Publishers. It was a door of opportunity that was completely opened by the Lord. I was the first African American that the company had ever hired and working in their customer service department would prove to be both extremely challenging and stressful. Women owned the company and I had never worked for such powerful and wealthy women in my life. The CEO had started the company out of the trunk of her car and in a few years, it had become quite successful. My immediate co-workers were all so different from what I was accustomed to. My supervisor was a follower of New Age. There were at least two Catholics, a Seventh-day Adventist and a few others who claimed nothing. I tell you, God put me in the middle of the real world! Gone was my being surrounded by people who had the same beliefs that I did.

And then it happened. I had been with the company for the better part of three years and the CEO was to retire. Her retirement party was a dinner cruise out of the Boston harbor. They sent a bus to the work place to pick us all up and take us to the harbor and for the next four hours, we were surrounded by the elite. There were doctors, lawyers, authors, and successful sales representatives. And there I was little insignificant me wondering how a woman who had grown up in the projects in Norfolk, Virginia, found herself on a dinner cruise sailing out of the Boston Harbor. I was the only African American on the entire ship! I even looked for a waiter that perhaps looked like me--not! "Oh, God you said it! Now how do I minister to these people? Do I tap my glass and ask for their attention? Do I stand on my chair and by faith just say what comes to my mind?" Needless to say, I did nothing but enjoy myself that night.

Shortly thereafter, my time at Sundance ended as we were preparing for our next transfer assignment to Germany. My co-workers gave me a farewell dinner at my favorite Chinese restaurant and there were no people of renown at my farewell, just the regular folks that I worked with, on a day-to-day basis. At the end of the meal, I was given the opportunity to go from person to person and tell them what each of them meant to me. And you guessed it; the anointing of God was so strong that there was not a dry eye in the place.

The next morning, I questioned the Lord about ministering to those doctors and lawyers and people of renown thinking that while on that ship I had missed an open door. I told the Lord that I just did not understand. And he spoke to me ever so gently, "Vera you didn't miss it. You did minister to them. You ministered by how you lived before them. Your life was your testimony of me." Have you ever had the King of glory say something to you so full of His love that it humbled you to the very core of your being? I learned something that morning that has stayed with me throughout the years. And it is this, that those methods of ministry that we've learned are never to be written in concrete. The Holy Spirit is so creative and He is the one who will teach us what it really means to minister. Our job is to stay prepared by staying in close fellowship with the Father so that at a moment's notice the light of his love will so shine in us that men everywhere will see our good works and glorify the one in whom we believe and trust for eternal life. This book is not written to be a blueprint for ministry. If that is what you are looking for then this book is not for you. But if you are looking for a window into how we are saved to be led by the Spirit of God in reaching others with a clear understanding that our salvation experience may not be the beginning of our lives but it is the beginning of truly living. And that we, who are believers, are all called to win those who are lost and to serve and it may not be in the way that we imagine; then this study is for you. If you are looking for more understanding in this process that we all must go through to become effective servants, then this study is for you. My prayer is that you would, prayerfully, study and allow the Holy Spirit to make you and use you in ways that you never thought possible.

HOW TO USE THE STUDY COMPANION AND JOURNAL

The Making study companion and journal has been incorporated in this book. The study companion has been designed to assist the reader in discovering their life purpose, and allowing God through His word and the inward working of the Holy Spirit to bring about the necessary changes needed to be progressively "made" to become effective in the fulfillment of that purpose.

It can be used either in a small group setting or by an individual during personal devotional and study times. It can be readily adapted to both.

Each chapter is formatted in the same manner, as it will contain the following four sections:

- ❖ Chapter Narrative and Commentary
- ❖ Study Questions
- ❖ Practicum (A practical exercise involving the theme of the chapter)
- ❖ Alone with the Father/Journaling (What the Lord, personally, speaks to you.)

If you are the leader or facilitator in a small group, setting it is suggested that you do more intensive study to be able to supply more information than is given in the narrative and commentary section of each chapter. You would then lead the group allowing them to, voluntarily, give their answers to the questions.

Before you begin please:

- ❖ Pray that God would give you revelation and show you ways to apply what you will learn in a very practical manner. Learning is one thing, but application solidifies what we learn.
- ❖ Read the passages of Scripture suggested more than once to get a clearer understanding of what is being conveyed.

During your study:

❖ Write down your answers as it will aid in memory retention. When you read, then write and then recite, you are more apt to retain.

❖ Don't forget to write what you gleaned from your personal time with the Lord in the journaling section. God will speak to you and it will be a joy going back at the end of the study and reflecting on what He spoke to your heart.

❖ Finally, always remember that confidentiality is a must! **Those very personal things that are discussed in your group stay within the group!**

INTRODUCTION

I was conceived in the mind of God before I was conceived in my mother's womb. I lived in her womb for 9 months and on a cold wintry Wednesday morning in 1955 I entered the world, kicking and screaming. I was not a stillbirth but classified as a live birth and for the next twenty-eight years I lived my life as best I knew how. It would be in my twenty-ninth year of living that I would find out that prior to that I had merely existed. I really began to live my life when I became born again. Now mind you, it was not wasted time because every day of my life God was watching me and caring for me, and setting a path for me. He would place people in my life to help me and every experience would be used for His ultimate purpose for my life. God waste nothing, not people nor resources nor time.

God specifically designed each of us on purpose with purpose. We all go through a process of being, "made" so that we can be most effective in executing His purpose for our lives. Isn't it a sad thought that millions upon millions of His creatures live aimlessly not fulfilling the purpose that He has for them, because they choose not to serve Him. The first and most important thing that a person can ever do is to make the choice to completely surrender their lives to the working of the Holy Spirit and be born again.

The process of being made, sculpted, fashioned by the hand of God will prove to be a lifelong process. However, if we are to be truly effective for Kingdom work we must allow ourselves to be placed on the potter's wheel repeatedly. It will not feel good and at times, we may even object to His methods. We must remember that there is no better place to be, but securely in the will of God, walking in obedience to His will and living the best, most effective lives that we can.

During this process, it will mean having integrity ingrained in us and learning that genuine accountability is our friend and not our enemy. To live for God is the single most important decision that we could ever make! To live an effective life for God will bring eternal reward beyond what we could ever imagine - guaranteed. Your mission, if you choose to accept it, is to stay on God's wheel and allow Him to sculpt you into the vessel of His choosing. It's trusting time!

CHAPTER ONE

First Thing's First
"I Am Responsible For My Own Choices"

The Lord does not delay and is not tardy or slow about what He promises, according to some people's conception of slowness, but He is long-suffering (extraordinarily patient) toward you, not desiring that any should perish, but that all should turn to repentance 2 Peter 3: 9 Amplified Version.

It is not through the will of God that anybody end up in hell. His desire is that all would be with him forever. It is sad to say that although He extends the invitation to all, not all will accept it, and some will leave this world, as we know it for an eternity of torment that was not meant for them. Judgment delayed does not mean that judgment is not coming. You choose to go to hell or not! It is your choice. We must not automatically assume that everyone who reads this book is born again. Therefore, it is imperative that we talk about this life changing experience called salvation. It is so worth it to tell anyone and everyone who will listen about the tremendous price paid for every human being on the planet, and that salvation is available to all.

Let me explain how God wooed me to make the right choice. Recently, I made a visit back to the place where I was born and raised after being away for quite a few years. I was astonished at how everything had changed so drastically and it was very trying to find my way around town. Driving around into the neighborhood where I lived from ages 6 to 12, I was disappointed to find that much of the neighborhood had been demolished. All that remained was the elementary school I attended and the Lutheran Church where I first heard about Jesus Christ. The members of this church would come into my neighborhood and, with the permission of my parents, take me to church. I remember viewing a filmstrip that told about the crucifixion and the resurrection of Jesus Christ. It was during the Easter season. For years and years, those images would remain in my mind. Also in our neighborhood, there was an elderly woman who lived in the back of us named Mrs. Turner. Mrs. Turner would put out little chairs in her back yard and invite us kids over for cookies and Kool-Aid and share stories from the Bible. I remember her telling us about Jonah and the whale and Noah's ark. God used this precious woman to water the seed of his word that had already planted in my heart. In 1 Corinthians 3:5-7, the Apostle Paul writes to the Christians in Corinth concerning quarrels they were having as to whom they would follow or who was greatest amongst them and deserved their following. *"What, after all, is Apollos? And what is Paul? Only servants, through whom you came to believe — as the Lord has assigned to each his task. I planted the seed, Apollos watered it, but God made it grow. So, neither he who plants nor he who waters is anything, but only God, who makes things grow"* (Amplified Version). It was those precious people in the Lutheran Church whom God used to plant His seed in my heart; Mrs. Turner watered that seed and God was the one to make it grow. Throughout the years leading up to my true conversion, there would be countless others whom God would send my way to continue to water what had been planted within me. For the next 23 years I would become religious. I even got baptized when I was twelve. But it wasn't until I was 29 years old and a new-found friend invited me to a spiritual crusade that I repented of my sins and asked Jesus to come into my heart and be Lord of my life.

In Saint John the 3rd chapter Jesus told the Pharisee, Nicodemus, *"Most assuredly, I say to you, unless one is born again, he cannot see the kingdom of God.* Jesus went on to say that, *'Most assuredly, I say to you, unless one is born of water and the Spirit, he cannot enter the Kingdom of God.'"* Hmmm, so what was the Lord saying concerning this being born of water and the Spirit? Is it probable that he meant that one is regenerated by the Holy Spirit of God and then must be baptized to make his or her salvation complete? Is it probable that he meant that as he hung on the cross (the crucifixion) and he was pierced in his side and water and blood came out that it pointed the way to salvation whether one was baptized in water? I truly believe that salvation is not complicated or hard to understand if we receive what we hear by faith. We must first believe that God is exactly who He says He is. Some things are just beyond our understanding. Have you ever had a child to ask you, "Where did God come from?" God, from the day we come into existence, is constantly revealing to us who He is and He created us with freedom of choice to either accept or reject that revelation. The word of God says *that there is none righteous, no not one* (Romans 3:10). No one is born in right standing with God. He is the only one who can put us in right standing with himself. He reveals to us that *all have sinned and have come short of his glory* (Romans 3:23). Why? It was through the initial sin of Adam that eternal damnation passed to all men (Romans 5:12). That means that every living and breathing human being on the planet is born into sin and all need a Savior. We are further told that the payment for that sin is death and that God has made a way for us to be reconciled back to himself through the gift of his son Jesus Christ (Romans 6:23). And it was Christ who died for us simply because He loved us (Romans 5:8). And all we must do is, by faith, accept the fact that He did die for us, and that God raised him from the dead and confess or acknowledge this belief, repent of our sins and call upon the name of the Lord (ask Him to come into our hearts and we shall be saved or born again (Romans 10: 9-17). Some are saying that all roads lead to God; whether it is Buddhism, Islam, or New Age etc. But unless they make the claim that Jesus Christ is the only way to the heart of the Father, then it is a wrong road. It is a road that is called the path of deception. The Qur'an does not believe Jesus to be the son of God, but one of the five Major Prophets sent by God to give guidance. Islam denies the death and resurrection of Jesus Christ. The New Agers refer to Jesus as the Master Jesus and believe that he had previous incarnations. Buddhist, take no particular view of Jesus. But Jesus, himself said, "*I am the Way and the Truth and the Life; no one comes to the Father except by (through) Me* John 14:6 (Amplified Version).

I do not know where or when, exactly, that I first heard the statement, "My life is a gift from God, and what I do with my life is my gift back to Him." But throughout the years this statement has become a lifelong quest for me. You see, one day I woke up from the stupor of living a life without Jesus being Savior and Lord of my life. That day I finally decided that I wanted to be different and to live differently. I got sick and tired of being sick and tired of searching for answers and finding none. That has been more than 33 years ago that I believed and accepted what God had been trying to tell me all along concerning His Son. On that day, I went from religion to relationship in an instant and my life has never been the same! My only regret is that I waited so long to give my heart, my life, my everything to Him. And to know that He waited on me, all the time wooing me to give me the very best that He had to offer, is mind boggling! Oh, such love the Father had and has for me! It is almost too much to comprehend! I need the Lord so much. I needed Him so much more than I even knew. He was the One who gave my life meaning and He was the One who told me who I was. It was He who affirmed me and filled me with so much of Himself that I could hardly breathe! He is my everything. Now who wouldn't want to be saved by such a One as He? He chose me and then I chose Him.

Those of us who have been saved by grace have become a participant in a divine sisterhood whereby we did not have to take a secret oath or pledge or go through a rigorous initiation process to become a member. It is quite humbling to receive something that you know that you did not do one thing to deserve and yet you received it anyway. So, if by chance, you have never decided to accept the Lord Jesus Christ as your very own personal Savior; now is the time to do just that. Be forewarned, every excuse under the sun will come to your mind as to why you cannot or you should not make the decision to follow Christ. The bottom line is this, you need the Lord more than you can imagine in your life right now; He loves you and wants to give you the very best that He has to offer. You might even say, "I'm a good person." Guess what? Your good could never ever be good enough! It is by His grace that we are saved and not by our good works.

Now, if you have already made the most important decision of your life and you are already a child of the King then we need to be about the business of letting our light so shine before men that they see our good works and bring glory to the Father. ... We are responsible for our own choices. All of us will one day stand before the Father and give an account of the deeds done in this life. And thank God that the most important thing that we could ever do is to make sure that our names are written in the Book of Life (Luke 10:17-20). Hallelujah, my name is in the Book! Is your name in the Book?

THE MAKING

STUDY QUESTIONS

Before you begin attempting to answer the following questions, please take time and prayerfully read Genesis 1:1 – 3:24 The History of Creation/Life in the Garden/The Temptation and the Fall of man.

1. After reading the account of the history of creation, what does it tell you about the character of God?

_____

_____

_____

_____

2. In your own words write what you imagine life was like in the Garden of Eden for Adam and then for Adam and Eve.

_____

_____

_____

_____

3. What was God's original plan for humankind?

_____

_____

_____

_____

4. Explain what effect the fall of man had on humankind.

_____
_____
_____
_____
_____

God made a way: Look up the following Old Testament Scriptures concerning the Messiah (The Anointed One).

Born in Bethlehem (Ephratah)	Micah 5:2
Born of a virgin	Isaiah 7:14
Priest after order of Melchizedek	Psalm 110:4
He would perform many miracles.	Isaiah 35: 5-6
He would open blinded eyes.	Isaiah 29:18
He will speak in parables.	Psalm 78:1-2
Gentiles would believe in Him, while the Jews would reject Him.	Isaiah 8:14, 28:16, 60:3; Psalm 22:7-8, 118:22
A messenger (man of wilderness) will prepare way for Him.	Isaiah 40:3; Malachi 3:1
He would enter Jerusalem riding a donkey.	Zechariah 9:9
He would be hated for no reason.	Psalm 69:4
He would be betrayed.	Psalm 41:9
Price of betrayal 30 pieces of silver	Zechariah 11:12
He would be beaten, spat upon.	Isaiah 50:6
Pierced	Zechariah 12:10

Crucifixion	Psalm 22, Psalm 34:20
Resurrected from the dead	Psalm 16:10
Ascend into heaven	Psalm 68:18
Seated at the right hand of God	Psalm 110:1
Son of God	Psalm 2:7

Now look up the following New Testament Scriptures of the fulfillment of the Old Testament prophecies concerning the Messiah.

Born in Bethlehem (Ephrathah)	Luke 2:4-20
Born of a virgin	Matthew 1/ Luke 1
Priest after order of Melchizedek	Hebrews 5:6
He would perform many miracles.	John 2:1-11, 6:16-21, 11:1-45; Matthew 8: 23-27, 9: 18, 23-26
He would open blinded eyes.	Matthew 9:27-31, 12:22, 20:29-34; Mark 8:22-26, 10:46-52; Luke 18:35-43; John 9:1-7
He will speak in parables.	Matthew 13:34
Gentiles would believe in Him, while the Jews would reject Him.	1 Peter 2:7-8
A messenger (man of wilderness) will prepare way for Him.	Matthew 3:1-3; 11:10; John 1:23; Luke 1:17
He would enter Jerusalem riding a donkey.	Matthew 21:4-9; Luke 19:32-37
He would be hated for no reason.	John 15:25
He would be betrayed.	Matthew 27:3-10
Price of betrayal 30 pieces of silver	Matthew 27:3-10
He would be beaten, spat upon.	Matthew 26:67, 27:26-30
Pierced	John 19:34

Crucifixion	John 19:16-37
Resurrected from the dead	John 20: 1-18; Acts 2:31
Ascend into heaven	Acts 1:9
Seated at the right hand of God	Acts 7:56; Hebrews 1:3
Son of God	Matthew 3:17

5. Who is Jesus Christ?

_____

_____

_____

6. What does it mean for a person to be born again? Read John 3 in its entirety and before answering the question.

_____

_____

_____

_____

_____

7. Explain God's plan of salvation. Read Romans 3:10, 1:23, 5:12, 6:23, 5:8 and 10:9-17.

_____

_____

_____

_____

_____

8. Define the word choice.

9. Read Galatians 6:7. What does this scripture have to do with the choices that we make?

10. Have you made a choice to become a follower of Jesus Christ? If the answer is no, why not? If the answer is yes, when, where and how did you make that choice?

11. Explain, in your own words, "My life is a gift from God and what I do with my life is my gift back to Him."

PRACTICUM

Partner with someone and tell him or her "Who" Jesus Christ is and why you have made a choice to serve Him. When you have done this practicum, fill in the date of completion _____ and the name of the person that you partnered with _____. Now write down what you gleaned from the execution of this practicum.

_____
_____
_____
_____
_____
_____
_____
_____
_____
_____
_____
_____
_____
_____
_____
_____
_____

THE MAKING

ALONE WITH THE FATHER

CHAPTER TWO

A Walking Sermon
"I Am a Living Epistle"

You are our epistle written in our hearts, known and read by all men; clearly you are an epistle of Christ, ministered by us, written not with ink but by the Spirit of the living God, not on tablets of stone but on tablets of flesh, that is, of the heart 2 Corinthians 3: 2-3.

If I ever had to reflect on what my ultimate purpose in life is, I am convinced that it is to worship and live for God in whose image I was created. In addition, my purpose in life is to convince others that they too have purpose. It sounds a bit monumental, doesn't it? Well, it is not with the Helper, the Comforter, and the Counselor actively living and working on the inside of those who belong to the Father. He is the One who helps us to know what our purpose is in life and to live out that purpose. Whew! I am so glad that I do not have to go at this on my own, aren't you?

The Apostle Paul wrote his second letter to the saints in Corinth, regarding them having been influenced by false teachers. These false teachers had come into the assembly of believers and tried to pit the saints against Paul. In turn, Paul sent Titus to them to deal with the problem, which led some to reconsider the messages that Paul had taught. We can see that Paul, continually expressed his thanks to the ones who had reconsidered and he continued to try to convince the others who had not.

So what was the Apostle Paul saying when he referred to the saints at Corinth as an epistle of Christ? What did it mean when he stated that their lives were a letter not written with ink but by the Spirit of the living God read by all men? Well, let's try and figure it out. Are you ready to dive into the Word and believe God for revelation after revelation? I know I am. Here we go!

Recently, I began teaching a Bible study on the Epistle to the Romans. In the first chapter I came across something so interesting that I needed a bit more clarification. It was Romans 1:18-19, *"For the wrath of God is revealed from heaven against all ungodliness and unrighteousness of men, who suppress the truth in unrighteousness, because what may be known of God is manifest in them, for God has shown it to them."* These two verses of scripture, I learned are a beginning of the explanation of God's wrath against all unrighteousness and ungodliness. Since creation God has made himself known, therefore the ungodly and the unrighteous have no excuse. In other words, those who do not belong to God cannot use denial of His existence as an excuse for not serving Him. However, the question remained, "How and why did they suppress the truth of God?" So, I went all the way back to the beginning and read Genesis 1: 26-27 *"Let us make man in Our image, according to Our likeness; let them have dominion over the fish of the sea, over the birds of the air, and over the cattle, over all the earth and over every creeping thing that creeps on the earth. So God created man in His own image; in the image of God He created him; male and female He created Him."* Then I went to Genesis 2:7 *"And the Lord God formed man of the dust of the ground, and breathed into his nostrils the breath of life and man became a living being."*

The word image in the Hebrew is tselem and was used as in images of tumors, mice, heathen gods. It also meant likeness (of resemblance) and it further meant semblance. The modern-day definition of image is a reproduction of the form of a person or object, especially a sculptured likeness. To sculpture means to fashion into a three-dimensional figure. So then, an image can be defined as a three-dimensional likeness of something or someone. Wow, we are created to be a three-dimensional representation of God! We are created to be like God but we are not God! To dimension is to cut or shape specifically as in length, width, and height. God deliberately, purposefully, and specifically created us in His image. When Moses wrote Genesis, it was during the time when the people had been under Egyptian bondage and the only tangible image of God they had was Pharaoh. Pharaoh saw himself as a god and therefore had many images or little sculptures made in his image. However, the sculptures of this false god, Pharaoh, were made with the hands of men and could be tossed away if no longer useful. I can see that God intended for us to know and understand that we were fashioned by Him the creator of the universe. He was the One who spoke everything into existence, which meant that every human being on the planet (whether saved or unsaved) has value and worth as all were created in His image! The fact that he took dirt (clay) to fashion man speaks of the frailty of man. That frailty should serve to keep all humanity humble, but, unfortunately, it does not. I further understand that as we were created in the image of God-God the Father,

God the Son and God the Holy Spirit; we were created with a spirit, a soul, and a body. The bodies that we live in are the physical houses for our souls and our spirits. We are spiritual beings as we received the breath of God, who possesses a soul (we think, we have a personality and freedom of choice) and we live in a physical body (earthly body that include five senses: taste, touch, sight, smell, and hearing). In the beginning, humankind did not have clothes made by the hand of man but were clothed with the glory of God. Nakedness, back then was glorious! Can you imagine that when all of creation looked at that first man they truly did see a reflection of the Godhead? Now let us move ahead through the ions of time.

When the Apostle Paul wrote the epistle to the Romans, he stated that the ungodly and unrighteous suppressed the truth of who God was even though they were created in His image. And after revisiting and pondering the creation of man, I was reminded of Matthew 5:13-16: *"You are the salt of the earth; but if the salt loses its flavor, how shall it be seasoned? It is then good for nothing but to be thrown out and trampled underfoot by men. You are the light of the world. A city that is set on a hill cannot be hidden. Nor do they light a lamp and put it under a basket, but on a lampstand, and it gives light to all who are in the house. Let your light so shine before men that they may see your good works and glorify your Father in heaven."* Jesus said that we are salt. Now let us example the characteristics of salt:

- **<u>Salt is a preservative.</u>** Salt prevents spoiling. Salt is rubbed into or onto meat to keep it from going bad or from becoming completely rotten. God's people are needed in this world to keep it from sliding further and further into the stench of sin. We are in the world but not of the world. We must live in this world but we are not to be completely or absolutely subject to the world system.

- **<u>Salt adds flavor.</u>** Cooks will add salt as a seasoning to enhance the natural flavor of the food. Without salt added, the food would be tasteless. As saints of God, we add the seasonings of love, joy, peace, and hope (to name a few) that make for a better life no matter how dire the world is right now. See Jeremiah 29:11-13.

- **<u>The color of salt is white.</u>** In Christendom, the color white stands for purity. We are to live pure lives. See James 4:4, Romans 12:2 and James 1:27 and 1 Peter 4:4.

- **<u>Salt is used as fertilizer.</u>** Fertilizer promotes the growth of food. As salt, we promote the growth of that which is good going from glory to glory and from faith to faith. We are to shun evil and cling to what is good!

- **Salt creates thirst.** The word of God tells us that those who hunger and thirst after righteousness shall be filled. Our lives, the way the world sees us live, is supposed to create a thirsting after the things of the Kingdom. The question is then, "Does my life make anyone thirsty for the things of God?"

So, is it safe to say that salt loses all of its good qualities when it becomes one with the world? "...*But if salt loses its flavor, how shall it be seasoned*"?

Jesus said that we are the light of the world. To function as the light of the world, we are to be the guides who lead the world to Jesus, who is the greatest light! I heard a young man preach recently about the light of the moon in comparison to that of the sun. He stated that both the sun and the moon give off light, but the light that the moon gives off is a direct reflection of the light of the sun.

- We are the light in all this darkness. See Proverbs 4:18 and Ephesians 5:8-9
- Jesus Christ is the greatest light. See 2 Corinthians 4:4-6
- We are to be that light or guide that leads to Jesus. See John 3:19-21
- We are to be reflectors of His light. See Acts 26:17-18 and 1 Peter 2:9

Our purpose is to be empowered by God to do good works, that men would see those good works, and bring glory to Him.

Now back to Romans and the question that I pondered earlier, "How did they suppress the truth of who God is, even though they are created in His image? The answer is that they suppressed the truth by their unrighteous/disobedient living. Even though they were created in His image, they did not bring glory to God by either what they did or did not do. When we do not live as God purposes, then the truth about the God we serve is suppressed by our unrighteousness (by us not doing what is right)/disobedience!

I have often heard the expression, "We are the only Bible that some people may ever read." We, as saints of God, have a responsibility to live the very best life in God that we possibly can. The Father expects it of us. If we love Him and if He is all that He claims to be, then why wouldn't we want to be like Him? Small children absolutely love to imitate adults, especially their moms and dads. As little girls, we like to play dress up and put on our mothers' clothes and high heels and make-up and have pretend tea parties. Or we play mommies by taking care of our dolls. We pretend to feed them and change their diapers and coddle them when they cry. We do all those things that we have seen our mommies do. How much more should we do the things that we know the Father has done? Yes, we are living letters written by the hand of God. What is the world reading when they witness our lives? I don't know about you but I want to be an express image of the love of God. I want to truly be a reflector of the greatest light, Jesus Christ! I want to be good and to do good by His grace so that the good that I do will lead others directly to Him.

STUDY QUESTIONS

1. In your own words, write what you believe is your purpose in life.

_____
_____
_____
_____
_____

2. Read John 16:5-15 before answering the following question. What did Jesus say about the work of the Holy Spirit?

_____
_____
_____
_____
_____
_____

3. Look up definitions for the following words: dimension, representation, deliberate, purpose, and specific and write them below.

_____
_____
_____
_____
_____

4. Read Romans 1 and Genesis 1 and 2 before answering the following questions. What does it mean to be created in the image of God? And, who did God create in His image?

___

5. Paul said, *"For the wrath of God is revealed from heaven against all ungodliness and unrighteousness of men, who suppress the truth in unrighteousness, because what may be known of God is manifest in them, for God has shown it to them."* Please give at least one explanation of how this possibly could be done.

___

6. Please explain the characteristics of salt and how it relates to the believer.

___

7. Explain how we are the light in this world and give a scripture reference for your answer.

8. After having read the commentary and answered all the questions; write, again what you feel that your purpose in life is and how the Lord is helping you to live out your purpose.

PRACTICUM

Find someone this week and explain to them the purpose of your life and after you have done so write down the immediate results.

THE MAKING

ALONE WITH THE FATHER

CHAPTER THREE

Epiphany of Purpose
"Up-close and Personal"

The word of the Lord came to me, saying, "Before I formed you in the womb I knew you, before you were born I set you apart; I appointed you as a prophet to the nations" Jeremiah 1:4-5.

From the time I was 16 years old and I signed up to be a candy striper in our local community hospital, I wanted to be a nurse. It gave me almost unexplainable pleasure to help those who were in need. I set out to become the best nurse that I could by taking the courses that would help get me there. During my senior year, I had enough credits to go to high school in the morning and Vocational School in the afternoon for Licensed Practical Nursing. But through the course of my own rebellion and other circumstances beyond my control, I dropped out of school for a time. I would eventually go back and complete my senior year within a few months. However, I did not re-enroll in nursing school but went into the United States Air Force instead. Upon enlistment, I thought that I could go to school to become a medic or at least be assigned a job in the medical field that would eventually be a road that would lead me back to nursing. They assigned me Veterinary Services. Imagine that! To this day I do not care for animals as pets. I did, however, come to love other aspects of the job that included Food and Sanitation inspection and later Environmental Medicine. The almost twelve years that I spent in the Air Force were a blessing to me. Some of the skills that I learned I still use today and I am so grateful for having served my country.

The year was 1999 and I had arrived back in Germany for a second time. One morning I was in my office seeking the Lord and asking him if my life had any meaning. At the time, I had been in my relationship with Him for 14 years, was called to teach His word and had been trained and used in many different ministerial positions. My mind went back to the nursing profession and I questioned the Lord about the desire that I knew he had put in me at an early age. I asked the Lord if I had missed it, and if I had, perhaps it was not too late to go back to school and fulfill the original purpose that He had for my life. Maybe I was not just to be a teacher of the word but I was also to be become a nurse and to teach others to become nurses also. I was feeling rather anxious about it when I heard the Lord say, "Go look up the definition for nurse in the dictionary." I did and the definition said that a nurse was a person educated and trained to care for the sick or disabled (www.thefreedictionary.com). Then he asked me, "Who does a nurse assist?" I said, "the doctor." Then he asked me, "Am I not the Great Physician? You have not missed your calling, continue to walk with me!" I broke down and just wept. Oh yes, I was a big cry baby that day and many days since when the Lord has had to remind me of my purpose and the plan that He has for my life. As I write this chapter I have just finished reading two 500 plus page Christian novels and I read them within a week's time. By the way when I was called to be a teacher of the Word the Lord emphatically told me that the love for reading that I had; He had placed that in me. Imagine that! This morning I was praying and talking to the Lord about the author of those two novels and how much I admired her writing. I prayed that He would use my writing as well to touch someone's heart as my heart was touched while reading those two Christian novels. The Lord then reminded me of all the poems and short stories that I had written in high school and how they were in a folder tucked away in my file, long forgotten. He reminded me of how the gift of writing was first given to my mom and then to me and to my daughter as well. Once again, I wept and thanked Him for the gift and He reminded me to keep on following His lead. I had an epiphany of purpose! A teacher, a spiritual nurse and a writer ... and to think that he could use little old me! It is one thing to know that you were created on purpose with purpose but it is an entirely different thing to have a sudden revelation in your innermost being of what that purpose is. Enough about me, now let us look at the prophet Jeremiah.

In the first chapter of the book of Jeremiah, we read about the calling of this great man of God. He said, *"The word of the Lord **came to me**. ..."* This lets us know that he personally heard from God. Oh, it is wonderful when the Lord speaks to us through his word, through others and sometimes even through circumstances, but it is most wonderful when we hear that still small voice of the Father in our inner most being. In John 10:27 we read, *"My sheep hear my voice, and I know them and they follow me."* It was Henry Blackaby who said in his book Experiencing God, *"God is always speaking, and we are just not always listening."* God will speak to us concerning our purpose in life. If He did it for Jeremiah, He will do it for each one of us. We have but to ask, listen, watch and wait.

The word that Jeremiah received from the Lord was, "Before I formed you in the womb I knew you; before you were born I sanctified you; I ordained you a prophet to the nations Jeremiah 1:5." Okay so the first thing that He said was, "Before I formed you in the womb I **knew** you." The word knew in the original Hebrew was the word (da, the transliterated word yada`, which meant to perceive and see and to acknowledge (www.blueletterbible.org). God was directly aware of our conception and He recognized us as a valid existence. We were created in the mind of the omniscient Father even before our parents came together and the miracle of conception took place. We did not or could not have chosen our parents. God knew who they would be and the circumstances surrounding our conception and we were not mistakes! We were chosen by the Father to exist on this planet. He has a purpose for our lives. He knew who our biological parents would be, including, race, body frame, culture, upbringing, etc. "Oh yes, you shaped me first inside, then out; you formed me in my mother's womb. I thank you, High God—you're breathtaking! Body and soul, I am marvelously made! I worship in adoration—what a creation! You know me inside and out, you know every bone in my body; you know exactly how I was made, bit by bit, how I was sculpted from nothing into something. Like an open book, you watched me grow from conception to birth; all the stages of my life were spread out before you, the days of my life all prepared before I'd even lived one day" Psalm 139:13-16 (The Message Bible). We were chosen on purpose to live out our purpose; right here, right now!

The next thing that He said to Jeremiah was, "Before you were born **I sanctified you…**" The word sanctified in the original Hebrew is #dq and the transliterated word is Qadash and its meaning is to be set apart, preparation (www.classic.studylight.org). Jeremiah knew what it meant to have a person (priesthood) set apart from the rest and declared holy by God for a specific purpose. Whether or not we were physically dedicated to the Lord by our parents, we, as children of God, have been chosen and set apart from the world for Kingdom work. Neither of my parents were saved when I was born and knew nothing as far as I know about dedicating children to the Lord and yet I know that I have been called by God, Himself and set apart from the world for Kingdom work and so have you.

The next thing that God said to Jeremiah was, "**I ordained you** a prophet to the nations." The word ordained in the original Hebrew is rcy and the transliterated word is yatsar. It means purposes, planned, predetermined (www.studylight.org). It was already predetermined and planned by God that

THE MAKING

Jeremiah would be a prophet to the nations. The primary job or assignment of the prophet was to call God's people back to being faithfully obedient to Him and to the exclusive worship of Him. During the course of Jeremiah living out the purpose for which he was born, he would be attacked by his own countrymen, beaten and put into stocks by the priest and the false prophet, imprisoned by the king, threatened with death and thrown into a cistern. The "Path of Purpose" may prove to be unbearable at times. "Prophet" was not a title for Jeremiah, it was his calling. It was a calling to purpose. It was a calling to destiny and it was not easy.

Now with all that said, let's get up close and personal concerning our own epiphany of purpose…

*The word of the Lord **came to me**…*

- **What this reveals about God:** God wants to speak to us concerning our own lives. He desires to reveal to us what He wants to do with our lives. He wants us to know that we belong to Him. He takes responsibility for our lives. He goes out of His way to reveal Himself to His children, continually. John 10: 14-16: *"I am the Good Shepherd. I know my own sheep and my own sheep know me. In the same way, the Father knows me and I know the Father. I put the sheep before myself, sacrificing myself if necessary. You need to know that I have other sheep in addition to those in this pen. I need to gather and bring them, too. They'll also recognize my voice. Then it will be one flock, one Shepherd (The Message Bible.)*

- **What this reveals about us:** As Gentiles (those who were not born Jews), we are the other sheep in the pen who have been gathered in and have become a part of the one flock! We heard his voice calling and we answered and He continues to speak and we are to continue to listen for His voice. God can and will speak a personal word to each of us concerning our purpose in this life.

Leonard Ravenhall
The greatest miracle that God can do today is to take an unholy man out of an unholy world, and make that man holy and put him back into that unholy world and keep him holy in it.

*Before **I formed you** in the womb **I knew you**…*

- **What this reveals about God:** God is our Creator. Genesis 1:26-27: God spoke: "Let us make human beings in our image, make them reflecting our nature So they can be responsible for the fish in the sea, the birds in the air, the cattle, and, yes, Earth itself, and every animal that moves on the face of Earth." God created human beings; he created them godlike, reflecting God's nature. He created them male and female. God blessed them: "Prosper! Reproduce! Fill Earth! Take charge! Be responsible for fish in the sea and birds in the air, for every living thing that moves on the face of Earth." God thought about us and carefully formulated our existence and the reason for our existence in His mind first even before our conception. He carefully and methodically decided who we would be and what He intended for us to do for Him. He knows every intricate detail of our lives. In fact, He knows more about us than we know about ourselves because it was He who wired us a certain way to operate to maximum performance.

- **What this reveals about us:** We are God's creation. We are God's masterpiece. We are His gifts to His world. We are uniquely His and no two of us are exactly alike. We cannot fool Him because He knows us too well.

*Before you were born **I set you apart**...*

- **What this reveals about God:** God is Holy. He created us to be holy and as His children He has declared us to be holy. He is the one who chose us and specifically declared that we are His and our lives are to be lived for His divine purpose.

- **What this reveals about us:** Holiness is not an option if you are a child of God. As obedient children, let yourselves be pulled into a way of life shaped by God's life, a life energetic and blazing with holiness. God said, "I am holy; you be holy."1 Peter 1: 15 (Message Bible). The Hebrew word for holiness is kadesh which means something that is separatedor cut off or set apart (www.studylight.org). Holiness is not ordinary. The word for holy in the New Testament is hagios and it also means set apart or to be separated for special use (www.studylight.org). This word is used in the entire Bible to refer to God, people and things. So then to be set apart means that we have been chosen by a Holy God and declared holy and separated from the world system to be used by Him in the world system for His Kingdom work. This was his purpose for us before we were even born!

"What do we mean by [the sovereignty of God]? We mean the supremacy of God, the kingship of God, the god-hood of God. To say that God is Sovereign is to declare that God is God. To say that God is Sovereign is to de-

clare that He is the Most High, doing according to His will in the army of Heaven, and among the inhabitants of the earth, so that none can stay His hand or say unto Him what doest Thou? (Dan. 4:35). To say that God is Sovereign is to declare that He is the Almighty, the Possessor of all power in Heaven and earth, so that none can defeat His counsels, thwart His purpose, or resist His will (Psa. 115:3). To say that God is Sovereign is to declare that He is "The Governor among the nations" (Psa. 22:28), setting up kingdoms, overthrowing empires, and determining the course of dynasties as pleaseth Him best. To say that God is Sovereign is to declare that He is the "Only Potentate, the King of kings, and Lord of lords" (1 Tim. 6:15). Such is the God of the Bible."
—A. W. Pink, The Sovereignty of God, chapter 1.

I appointed you *as a prophet to the nations.*

- **What this says about God**: God is sovereign! The Sovereignty of God means that all things are under his control and nothing can happen without his permission or direction. He has the right and the power to govern all things! God is the one who appointed Jeremiah. He had the right and the power to appoint him.

- **What this says about us:** To appoint means to elect or designate to fill an office or position. To ordain means to authorize and invest with ministerial authority (www.thefreedictionary.com). *God has selected each of us to fill a preordained position in life and has invested us with the ministerial authority to carry it out. A minister is simply a servant! It's in Christ that we find out who we are and what we are living for. Long before we first heard of Christ and got our hopes up, he had his eye on us, had designs on us for glorious living, part of the overall purpose he is working out in everything and everyone Ephesians 1:11-12 (The Message Bible).*

Have you had an epiphany yet? Now it is time to go a little deeper and make it even more personal.

STUDY QUESTIONS

Before answering the questions that follow; please read Jeremiah the first chapter in its entirety at least twice from at least two different translations.

1. Who was Jeremiah and what was God's plan for his life?

2. What was Jeremiah's objection to God's plan for his life?

3. Do you feel that his objection reflected fear or humility or both?

4. An excuse is argument raised to be released from obligation or duty. What was God's reaction to Jeremiah's excuse?

5. Read Romans 11:29. Write down what you believe this passage of Scripture is saying.

6. Turn to Jeremiah 29:11-13. In Jeremiah 29: 10-14 the Lord was speaking to Israel concerning their captivity in Babylon. How can we apply this to our lives today?

7. Define epiphany.

8. Read the following Scripture before filling in the blanks that follow: Genesis 1:26-28, Psalm 139: 13-16, Jeremiah 1: 4-5, Jeremiah 29: 11-13, 1 Peter 4:10 and Romans 12: 4-5.

9. In accordance with Genesis 1: 26-28…God says that I am

10. In accordance with Psalm 1: 26-28…God says that I am

_____
_____
_____
_____
_____
_____

11. In accordance with Jeremiah 1:4-5…God says that He

_____
_____
_____
_____
_____
_____

12. In accordance with Jeremiah 29: 11-13…God says He

_____
_____
_____
_____
_____
_____

13. In accordance with 1 Peter 4:10…I have

14. In accordance with Romans 12:4-5…I am

PRACTICUM

Spend time in praise and worship of the Father and then sit quietly in His presence and ask him about his plan concerning your life and write down what he tells you.

_____
_____
_____
_____
_____
_____
_____
_____
_____
_____
_____
_____
_____
_____
_____
_____

Take a spiritual gift survey. I recommend the, Discovering Your God Given Gifts by Don and Katie Fortune or Finding Your Spiritual Gifts by C. Peter Wagner. After taking the survey, share what you discover with a spiritual leader that you trust. Ask them to pray with you concerning the findings.

VERA LERAY WARNER

ALONE WITH THE FATHER

CHAPTER FOUR

The Making of Me

My brethren, count it all joy when you fall into various trials, knowing that the testing of your faith produces patience. But let patience have its perfect work, that you may be perfect and complete, lacking nothing James 1:24 NKJV.

Bummer! That could have possibly been the attitude of some of the saints to whom James addressed this epistle back in 49 AD. James, the half-brother of Jesus Christ who was a leader in the Jerusalem church and one who was well acquainted with persecution, wrote these words to first century believers. These believers had come to live in Gentile communities after being scattered abroad because of persecution. Yep, that's right, "Bummer." Bummer is a slang term that we use today to express frustration or disappointment. James encouraged people enduring persecution to choose joy instead of frustration. "James, you have got to be kidding, right?" No doubt James wrote the letter to help them understand the why and to give them instructions on the how. They tell us that it is easier to go through something when you understand why you must go through it.

There is a term, "Self-Made Man" and it means having achieved success or recognition by one's own efforts. It means having made it by one's self (www.thefreedictionary.com). As saints of God, we know anything we have done or will do that is considered successful or good is not done through our own power and strength. It is because of the grace of God working within us and through us. We are women being made or fashioned by the hand of the Father and it is an ongoing process. And how does He make us? He does it through the trials that He allows in our lives. Now back to the text from a different translation: *Consider it a sheer gift, friends, when tests and challenges come at you from all sides. You know that under pressure, your faith-life is forced into the open and shows its true colors. So, don't try to get out of anything prematurely. Let it do its work so that you become mature and well-developed, not deficient in any way (James 1: 2-4 The Message Bible).*

Notice that in both translations it states, ***when*** you fall into various trials-**when** tests and challenges come at you-not *if* but **when**! The word **when** is defined as: at the time that, as soon as or whenever (www.thefreedictionary.com). The **when** has to do with time. At whatever time in your life you find yourself faced with challenges that come from all sides, count it all joy. Consider it to be a very valuable and important time in your life. Why? Because that **gift** of testing is tailor made just for you and the purpose of it is to develop patience in you. In other words, that time of testing will help you to grow up, spiritually! Patience is the capacity to tolerate delay, trouble or suffering without getting angry or upset. Now let's chat about **delay**, **trouble** and **suffering** a bit.

Delay means that it comes later or slower than expected or desired. You have to wait. It means being put on hold. Lazarus, the brother of Mary and Martha, had taken ill so they sent for Jesus. Jesus was told that the one whom he loved (Lazarus) was sick. But Jesus, upon hearing the news, did not immediately go to see about him; he **delayed** his departure. He did not immediately go to his aid or rescue. During that time of **delay,** Lazarus died and was buried. When the Lord finally arrived, he was told that Lazarus had been in the tomb for four days. No one understood why Jesus **delayed** his departure, not the disciples, nor the sisters of Lazarus; only Jesus. But we know that this delay was so that the ultimate plan and purpose of God could come forth. So, what can we learn from this? Two things that can be learned are that **delay does not mean denial** and that **God is always working behind the scenes despite what we see in the natural and are experiencing at that moment**. They prayed that their friend and brother would not die, but live. **Just because what God has promised us does not come to pass immediately does not mean that it will not.** Perhaps He is saying, "Just hold on and wait a while." You have need of patience. You are not yet complete.

Trouble is defined as extreme anxiety, sorrow, or grief. It is distress, affliction, or need. Trouble is mental anxiety or anguish (thefreedictionary.com). Sometimes the strain of mental anguish can be so intense that immediate help is needed and will cause you to cry out, "Lord, if you don't help me right now I am going to lose my mind!" Let's look to Jesus as our example: *Then Jesus came with them to a place called Gethsemane, and said to the disciples, "Sit here while I go and pray over there." He took with Him Peter and the two sons of Zebedee, and He began to be* **sorrowful and deeply distressed***. Then He said to them, "My soul is* **exceedingly sorrowful***, even to death. Stay here and watch with Me." He went a little farther and fell on His face, and prayed, saying, "O My Father, if it is possible,* *let this cup pass from Me; nevertheless, not as I will, but as You will." Then He came to the disciples and found them sleeping, and said to Peter, "What! Could you not watch with Me one hour? Watch and pray, lest you enter into temptation. The spirit indeed is willing, but the flesh is weak." Again, a second time, He went away and prayed, saying, "O My Father, if this cup cannot pass away from Me unless I drink it, Your will be done." And He came and found them asleep again, for their eyes were heavy. He left them, went away again, and prayed the third time, saying the same words. Then He came to His disciples and said to them, "Are you still sleeping and resting? Behold, the hour is at hand, and the Son of Man is being betrayed into the hands of sinners. Rise, let us be going. See, My betrayer is at hand" (Matthew 26:36-46 King James Version).* We cannot even begin to compare the trouble that we go through with what our Lord endured on the night that he was betrayed. But from time to time, we may find ourselves having to deal with extreme anxiety, sorrow or grief. In this life, we will have trouble. In this life, things will not always go as planned. In this life, we will experience loss and sometimes the things that we go through will be so intense that it will feel like we cannot breathe. In the first chapter of Job we read that the sons of God, one day presented themselves before the Father and Satan came among them. The Father asked Satan from where did he come and Satan told him from going to and fro on the earth and from walking back and forth on it. Now I don't know about you, but I picture the devil on earth watching and scrutinizing God's creation to see how he can steal, kill and destroy them. But God is the One who will have the last say! *Then the Lord said to Satan, "Have you considered My servant Job, that there is none like him on the earth, a blameless and upright man, one who fears God and shuns evil?" So Satan answered the Lord and said, "Does Job fear God for nothing? Have You not made a hedge around him, around his household, and around all that he has on every side? You have blessed the work of his hands, and his possessions have increased in the land. But now, stretch out Your hand and touch all that he has, and he will surely curse You to Your face!" And the Lord said to Satan, "Behold, all that he has is in your power****; only do not lay a hand on his person"***. So Satan went out from the presence of the Lord (Job 1:8-12 KJV).* Job was about to go through the very trial of his life at the hand of the adversary and yet God is the one who set the boundaries of his trial. **Nothing, absolutely nothing touches me without having to have my Father's permission!** God allows us to go through trials to make us and not to kill us. He never ever takes his eyes off us during the entire process, even when we think that we will not survive it. Let's look at the story of the teacup to get a more candid example of this process:

There was a couple who took a trip to England to shop in a beautiful antique store to celebrate their 25th wedding anniversary. They both liked antiques and pottery, and especially teacups. Spotting an exceptional cup, they asked "May we see that? We've never seen a cup quite so beautiful."

As the lady handed it to them, suddenly the teacup spoke, "You don't understand. I have not always been a teacup. There was a time when I was just a lump of red clay. My master took me and rolled me, pounded and patted me over and over and I yelled out, 'Don't do that. I don't like it! Let me alone.' But he only smiled, and gently said, 'Not yet! Then WHAM! I was placed on a spinning wheel and suddenly I was spun around and around and around. 'Stop it! I'm getting so dizzy! I'm going to be sick,' I screamed. But the master only nodded and said quietly 'Not yet.'"

"He spun me and poked and prodded and bent me out of shape to suit himself and then... Then he put me in the oven. I never felt such heat. I yelled and knocked and pounded at the door. Help! Get me out of here! I could see him through the opening and I could read his lips as he shook his head from side to side, 'Not yet.'"

"When I thought I couldn't bear it another minute, the door opened. He carefully took me out and put me on the shelf, and I began to cool. Oh, that felt so good! Ah, this is much better, I thought. But, after I cooled he picked me up and he brushed and painted me all over. The fumes were horrible. I thought I would gag. 'Oh, please, stop it, Stop it!' I cried. He only shook his head and said. 'Not yet!'"

"Then suddenly he put me back into the oven. Only it was not like the first one. This was twice as hot and I just knew I would suffocate. I begged. I pleaded. I screamed. I cried. I was convinced I would never make it. I was ready to give up. Just then the door opened and he took me out and again placed me on the shelf, where I cooled and waited - and waited, wondering "What's he going to do to me next?" An hour later he handed me a mirror and said, 'Look at yourself.' "And I did. I said, 'That's not me, that couldn't be me. It's beautiful. I'm beautiful!'"

Quietly he spoke: 'I want you to remember,' then he said, "I know it hurt to be rolled and pounded and patted, but had I just left you alone, you'd have dried up. I know it made you dizzy to spin around on the wheel, but if I had stopped, you would have crumbled. I know it hurt and it was hot and disagreeable in the oven, but if I hadn't put you there, you would have cracked. I know the fumes were bad when I brushed and painted you all over, but if I hadn't done that, you never would have hardened. You would not have had any color in your life. If I hadn't put you back in that second oven, you wouldn't have survived for long because the hardness would not have held. Now you are a finished product. Now you are what I had in mind when I first began with you."

Author Unknown

Suffer means to undergo or feel pain or distress. It means to sustain injury, disadvantage, or loss and at times having to endure it for long periods. (www.thefreedictionary.com). I remember being told early on in my walk with the Lord that when bad things happened to me it must be because I had sin in my life and I was the cause of my own suffering. But since developing in my relationship with the Lord, I have an entirely different perspective of suffering in the lives of God's people. I will be the first to admit that when I am going through a situation that causes suffering it is extremely hard to remember to pray for wisdom and understanding. Some things that I do are the direct cause of my pain and distress. Then there are other instances whereby I know that I have done absolutely nothing to bring pain upon myself. It is those times that what I am having to endure seems so unfair. I am reminded of the life of the Apostle Paul. Yes, he was a man specifically chosen by God as a minister to the Gentiles, but he was still an ordinary man chosen to do extraordinary things for the Kingdom of God and he suffered for it! *"I say again, let no one think me a fool. If otherwise, at least receive me as a fool, that I also may boast a little. What I speak, I speak not according to the Lord, but as it were, foolishly, in this confidence of boasting. Seeing that many boast according to the flesh, I also will boast. For you put up with fools gladly, since you yourselves are wise! For you put up with it if one brings you into bondage, if one devours you, if one takes from you, if one exalts himself, if one strikes you on the face. To our shame I say that we were too weak for that! But in whatever anyone is bold- speak foolishly—I am bold also. Are they Hebrews? So am I. Are they Israelites? So am I. Are they the seed of Abraham? So am I. Are they ministers of Christ?—I speak as a fool—I am more: in labors more abundant, in stripes above measure, in prisons more frequently, in deaths often. From the Jews five times I received forty stripes minus one. Three times I was beaten with rods; once I was stoned; three times I was shipwrecked; a night and a day I have been in the deep; in journeys often, in perils of waters, in perils of robbers, in perils of my own countrymen, in perils of the Gentiles, in perils in the city, in perils in the wilderness, in perils in the sea, in perils among false brethren; in weariness and toil, in* *sleeplessness often, in hunger and thirst, in fastings often, in cold and nakedness— besides the other things, what comes upon me daily: my deep concern for all the churches. Who is weak, and I am not weak? Who is made to stumble, and I do not burn with indignation"? 2 Corinthians 11:16-29 (New King James Version).* Wow, many of you going through this study cannot say that you have even come close to what this man of God had to endure and yet each of us can attest to periods whereas we have had to endure some things. And it would do us good to remember that **everything that God allows us to go through, the intention is to prepare us in our service for the Kingdom!** *Blessed be the God and Father of our Lord Jesus Christ, the Father of mercies and God of all comfort, who comforts us in all our tribulation, that we may be able to comfort those who are in any trouble, with the comfort with which we ourselves are comforted by God. For as the sufferings of Christ abound in us, so our consolation also abounds through Christ. Now if we are afflicted, it is for your consolation and salvation, which is effective for enduring the same sufferings which we also suffer. Or if we are comforted, it is for your consolation and salvation. And our hope for you is steadfast, because we know that as you are partakers of the sufferings, so also you will partake of the consolation 2 Corinthians 1: 3-7 (New King James Version).*

So then here are some points to remember as we are being made and fashioned and shaped by the hand of the Father:

- ❖ **When we experience delay**: Just because what God has promised us does not come to pass immediately does not mean that it will not.
- ❖ **When we experience trouble**: Absolutely nothing touches us without having to have our Father's permission!
- ❖ **When we find ourselves in the middle of circumstances that bring suffering in our lives**: Everything that God allows us to go through, the intention is to prepare us in our service for the Kingdom!

STUDY QUESTIONS

Before answering the following questions, please take a few minutes and read James 1: 1-12 at least five times and from at least five different translations.

1. When James wrote this epistle, to whom was he addressing it to and for what reason?

_____

_____

_____

_____

2. Look up the word persecution in a dictionary and write down its meaning.

_____

_____

_____

3. Do you feel that as Christians today we suffer persecution as did the first century saints? Give the reason for your answer.

_____

_____

_____

_____

4. Why are we to consider it a gift or joy when God allows us to be tested, tried, or challenged?

_____
_____
_____
_____
_____
_____

5. What does the term "Self-Made Man" mean?

_____
_____
_____
_____
_____
_____
_____

6. Record at least two verses of Scripture that emphasize our dependence upon God for everything.

_____
_____
_____
_____
_____
_____

7. As children of God, do we have a choice in whether we will go through trials? Give the reason for your answer.

8. One of the virtues that God really wants to cultivate in our lives is patience. Write down the definition of patience.

9. Now write down the definition of delay.

10. How do you think the following people were affected by the death of Lazarus?

Jesus

Mary/Martha

Friends/Neighbors

11. What does the name Lazarus mean?

12. What is the advantage of "delay" in the life of the Christian?

13. Reflect upon your own life. Now write down an experience whereby you believed God for something and you had to wait for what seemed like an eternity for it. Also write down what you gleaned from the waiting.

14. Now write down the definition of trouble.

___

Read Job 1-3 before answering the following questions.

15. Write down events in Job's life in chapters 1-3 that were a source of "trouble" in his life.

___

16. Now list statements of defeat and statements of encouragement from Job in chapters 1-3.

___

17. Now read Job 42: 1-17. What do you glean from reading about the end or completion of Job's trials?

_____
_____
_____
_____
_____
_____

18. After reading the story of the teacup, put into your own words how this story spoke to your heart.

_____
_____
_____
_____
_____
_____

19. Write down the definition of the word suffer.

_____
_____
_____
_____
_____
_____

20. After having read some of the sufferings that the Apostle Paul endured, how does it make you feel about your own personal walk with the Lord?

_____

_____

_____

_____

_____

_____

_____

21. Write down three key points to remember as we are being made by the Lord.

_____

_____

_____

_____

_____

_____

_____

THE MAKING

PRACTICUM

Do a timeline of your life recording those major events, both triumphs and tragedies. See example below…

```
Born 1959          First Day of School        Gave My Heart to the Lord
                        1964                          1970
```

Now write down how some of those major events had an impact on your life.

_____
_____
_____
_____
_____
_____
_____

How do you feel about your life right now?

_____
_____
_____
_____
_____
_____
_____

How do you want to be remembered when you have gone home to be with the Lord?

ALONE WITH THE FATHER

CHAPTER FIVE

Get the Little Foxes: A Study on Integrity

Catch for us the foxes, the little foxes that ruin the vineyards, our vineyards that are in bloom Song of Solomon 2:15 New International Version.

I was at a church service some years ago whereby the keynote speaker was Bob Larson, a renowned, worldwide deliverance minister. It was at this service that I first heard him use the phrase, 'Get your stuff before your stuff gets you!" Now stuff is defined as inward character, qualities or capabilities i.e. "she is made up of good stuff." Stuff is also worthless things i.e. clean the stuff out of the closet. And finally, stuff is defined as your personal property, your things, and your personal belongings. In this instance Bob Larson was referring to the personal, worthless things on the inside of us that have a negative effect upon our character that will eventually manifest as we act out or behave in a particular manner.

This chapter is about integrity in the life of the believer. It is about distinguishing between right and wrong conduct. It is about honesty and having the right motives and values.

We live in a world where, sad to say, civility (courtesy and politeness) is at an all-time low. Society at large is ungrateful, unmannered, and extremely prideful. Gone are the days when a hand shake was as good as your word. The norm has become to sign lengthy contracts and in the end, they still may not prove to be fool proof. It has become quite prevalent for people to search for loop holes to try and get out of honoring contracts. We, as a society, are becoming more and more skilled at making excuses. Lying and cheating are masquerading as excuses. It is as if our consciences have been seared with a hot iron and all that remains is a callus. Society has become insensitive and indifferent. But, this is not supposed to be said of the church. We are supposed to be quite different.

We live in a nation of professional liars. It has gotten to the point that our nation's leaders are not even expected to tell the truth. Most of them would not know the truth personified if it walked right up to them and bit them on the nose! But, this is not supposed to be said of the church. We are supposed to be quite different.

Integrity, is supposed to be so ingrained in the child of God that we just live it out without even giving it much thought. Let's examine this thing called integrity. Let's examine, in depth, three of its aspects: honesty, right motives and values. Let us begin with honesty.

❖ **Honesty** is defined as truthfulness, sincerity, freedom from deceit, uprightness and fairness. In the Bible, I can think of at least two men who are described as upright. The first one is Job, who was an honest man.

*There was a man in the land of Uz whose name was Job; and that man was blameless and **upright**, and one who [reverently] feared God and abstained from and shunned evil [because it was wrong] Job 1:1 Amplified Bible.*

There once was a man named Job who lived in the land of Uz. He was blameless— ***a man of complete integrity***. *He feared God and stayed away from evil Job 1:1 New Living Translation.*

The text says that Job was an "upright" man. Upright is translated from the Hebrew word yâshar, which means that he did what was ethically right (www.studylight.org). Now Job's name meant, "The hated or the persecuted one" and indeed he was hated by Satan and he was persecuted beyond what was imaginable! To the natural mind it would seem so unlikely that such an honorable, upright and virtuous man would have to go through so much as we would naturally equate right living with the absence of adverse circumstances. But the truth is that bad things do happen to decent, law abiding, ethical, moral people. Jesus said, *"I have told you all this so that you may have peace in me. Here on earth you will have many trials and sorrows. But take heart, because I have overcome the world John 16:33 New Living Translation."* God allowed Job, an upright man to suffer. God would use those intense trials to expose his weakness and sin and to also strengthen his faith. This is a lesson to us that God is always at work in us, removing those things that are offensive to him and strengthening those things in us that are in line with His character. We are a work in progress.

The next man that I want to mention is Simeon. *And behold, there was a man in Jerusalem, whose name was Simeon; and the same man was just and devout waiting for the Consolation of Israel and the Holy Ghost was upon him Luke*

2:25 New King James Version. At first it would seem as though we are not told too much about Simeon, unlike Job who would have a whole book written about his trials and triumphs. We only read a few verses about Simeon whose name means to be heard or hearing. What an honor for this upright man so moved by the Holy Spirit to proclaim the faithfulness of God. He was the man chosen by God to have eyewitness testimony of the arrival of the Messiah! Yes, God does reward the one who chooses to live a life of integrity.

So then, if honesty is uprightness and truthfulness, then dishonesty is deception and lying. In Acts the 5th chapter, we have the example of Ananias and Sapphira. They were a husband and wife team, who were property owners, sold some of it and brought a portion of the money from the sale to the disciples. But they crossed the line when they claimed that it was the whole amount. This was pre-meditated lying as it is obvious that he and his wife discussed what they were going to do before they did it and it cost them their lives! Peter told Ananias that it was Satan who had filled his heart and that he did not lie to man but to the Holy Spirit. Oh, that we would grasp that Satan is the father of lies and there is no truth in him and when we lie we are in fact yielding to the devil! Now on to right motives.

❖ **Right motives** are the object of my actions coming from what is right. The motivation for the action coming from an honest place and not tainted with selfish ambition or revenge. The question that we could ask ourselves is, "Is what is moving me to act coming from purity of heart and not tainted with selfish ambition or wanting to get revenge?" What motivated Ananias and Sapphira to lie? Perhaps it was selfish ambition as they wanted to appear to be someone whom they were not. *Psalm 139: 23-24 says, Search me O God, and know my heart; test me and know my anxious thoughts. Point out anything in me that offends you, and lead me along the path of everlasting life.* It is tough to ensure that our motives are coming from an honest place. It takes constantly cultivating a deep intimate relationship with the Lord so that when He convicts us; we are quick to accept the conviction, repent and purpose to do it right from that time onward. Now let's move on to values.

❖ **Values** are rules of right conduct. Through our values we show what we believe by how we live. This is where the hypocrite in us is flushed out! According to Merriam-Webster Dictionary, a hypocrite is a person who puts on a false appearance of virtue or religion or a person who acts in contradiction to his or her stated beliefs or feelings. It takes guts to be real! We hide out of fear of rejection. It is easier to hide than to be vulnerable and exposed. But if we say that we are Christians, a follower of Christ, one who identifies with Christ, to be Christ-like, then we have to work on being genuine even with our faults and short comings. Remember, as stated earlier we are a work in progress. 1 Peter 1:13-16 says, *"So think clearly and exercise self-control. Look forward to the gracious salvation that will come to you when Jesus Christ is revealed to the world. So you must live as God's obedient children. Don't slip back into your old ways of living to satisfy your own desires. You didn't know any better then. But now you must be holy in everything you do, just as God who chose you is holy. For the Scriptures say, "You must be holy because I am holy.""*

The world is watching! The children are watching but more importantly God is watching! I pray that this chapter is the beginning of you allowing God to bring you to a place in your life whereby you are known as a woman of your word! That you will be known as a woman of integrity! We are gardens in bloom and it is time to capture and put to death those "little foxes" that can ruin us.

STUDY QUESTIONS

Before answering the following questions please take time and read Acts 4:32-5:10 straight through without stopping. Then read again and underline or highlight key words and/or phrases that cause you to pause.

1. Describe the state of the believers in Acts 4:32-37.

_____
_____
_____
_____

2. Is this a picture of the Body of Believers today? Explain your answer.

_____
_____
_____
_____

3. Has the Lord ever nudged you to sell a possession and give away the proceeds? Has he ever had you to give a treasured possession away? How did it make you feel?

_____
_____
_____
_____

4. Who were Ananias and Sapphira?

5. Do you believe that they were true believers? Explain your answer.

6. What were at least two things that the Lord revealed about Ananias through Peter?

7. Sapphira was given the opportunity to be honest, and she was not. What does this say about her character?

8. What effect did what happen with Ananias and Sapphira have upon the other believers?

9. How does this make you feel concerning your own walk with God?

10. Write down the definition for integrity.

_____
_____
_____
_____
_____
_____
_____

11. Now explain the three aspects of integrity.

_____
_____
_____
_____
_____
_____
_____

Getting the "little foxes"

In the natural, it was the full-grown foxes that ate the fruit of the vine. It was the little foxes that not only ate the fruit, but the vine as well. Once the vine was destroyed, it could not bear fruit. In our lives, those little things that we allow to go unchecked can eventually become the cause of our downfall. It is time to get our stuff, before our stuff gets us!

12. You are in line at the grocery store. The cashier, in error, gives you more change back than you are supposed to get. What do you do? What does God say about this? Give a Scripture reference to support your actions.

13. You take your groceries to your car. Upon unloading them, you notice an item that the cashier did not charge you for. You have a pending appointment and if you take the time to return the item, you will be late for your appointment. What will you do? What does God say about this? Give a Scripture reference for your actions.

14. The phone rings and your husband or child answers it. It is for you. You whisper and tell them to tell the person who called that you are not at home. Is this okay? Why or why not? Give Scripture reference for your answer.

15. One of the elders of the church calls you and says that he needs someone to talk to as he is going through a tough time in his life right now. Elder Do-Good is a married man. What do you do? Give a Scripture reference for your actions.

_____
_____
_____
_____
_____

16. You are saved and single. You have been asked out on a date with Brother Willie. He takes you to a dinner and a movie and now you are standing at your front door. You live alone. What do you do next? Give Scriptural reference for your answer.

_____
_____
_____
_____
_____

17. You signed up to help with church clean-up. At the last minute, a friend has asked you to do something that you have wanted to do for a very long time. Both of things are scheduled for the same day at the same time frame. What do you do? Give Scriptural reference for your decision.

_____
_____
_____
_____
_____

18. After having answered the preceding questions, are there any areas in your life that you feel need a little work? If so write them down and repent for missing the mark and ask for the Father's help in becoming that woman of integrity that He intends for you to be. After all, you represent him to the world.

_____

_____

_____

_____

_____

_____

_____

_____

PRACTICUM

Everything that we do is to be motivated by our love for God. Pray and ask the Lord to direct you to at least three people that you can do something for, people that cannot compensate you for your service to them. After fulfilling your acts of love; write down how God directed you, what you did and how you feel about what you did. What was the outcome?

VERA LERAY WARNER

ALONE WITH THE FATHER

CHAPTER SIX

Accountability
I've Fallen and I Can Get Up

If we claim we have no sin, we are only fooling ourselves and not leaving in the truth. But if we confess our sins to him, he is faithful and just to forgive us our sins and to cleanse us from all wickedness. If we claim we have not sinned, we are calling God a liar and showing that his word has no place in our hearts 1 John 1: 8-10 New Living Translation.

It is inevitable that each of us will one day find ourselves having done something that has caused us to stumble and perhaps even fall in our walk with the Lord. We will have to come face to face with the fact that we have sinned and need forgiveness from God, from those whom we have sinned against and ourselves. Most everyday Christians are not apostles or prophets, or teachers or evangelists or pastors with large ministries whose sin when publicly exposed brings much reproach to the kingdom of God. No, we are just ordinary people that God choses from time to time to do extraordinary things for his Kingdom. Most of the time we are hidden away from the limelight and yet we are just as responsible for sin committed as those who are thrusted into the limelight. And yet, the word of God emphatically states that, "To whom much is given, much is required." This chapter is about the need for accountability in the life of every believer. It is about the cause and effect of the failure to accept and maintain accountability in the life of the believer. It is about how "healthy" accountability and forgiveness and restoration go hand in hand.

In the past couple of decades, the body of Christ has been faced with many scandals involving men and women of God who have found themselves entangled in a web of deceit that was patiently, methodically, and purposefully woven by the enemy. I was a new believer in 1987 when Jim Bakker resigned from Praise the Lord (PTL) after allegations of sexual misconduct, misappropriation, and fraudulent behavior involving donations in the excess of 165 million dollars. I must admit that I was not a frequent viewer of PTL. But when what had been done in the dark was brought to light, I was disappointed, angry and I hurt for the body of Christ, because as a young Christian, I knew that it would take more than a minute for us to regroup after this. Then a few days shy of exactly a year after this black eye, we were hit with another scandal involving Televangelist Jimmy Swaggart. This would touch me deeply as two weeks before the scandal hit the airwaves I was in my prayer closet one morning and the Lord impressed me to pray for Brother Swaggart and I remember questioning the Lord about it. I could not believe that God would use me, little insignificant me to pray for a man of such statue in the Christian community. But out of obedience I did pray and two weeks later his sin was exposed for the entire world to see. Imagine the impact this had upon my life. In the years preceding, his exposure I would get up every morning five days a week to view his broadcast, "Study in the Word." I can honestly say that I learned so much during those beginning years from his panel of scholars. I absolutely loved watching his revivals and camp meetings. I respected Brother Swaggart and his wife and the people that he surrounded himself with. But I did not worship him. So, when he fell, I did not fall with him, but I did go back into my prayer closet and I wept and wept and wept. I wept for him and his family and his church and the body of Christ and our nation. Because as young as I was in the Lord I knew that we had just gotten the other eye blackened by the enemy. In doing research for the writing of this chapter, I could go back and view on YouTube his tearful confession asking for forgiveness. Yet three years after this very public confession, his sin, that was obviously not dealt with, was exposed again and this time there was no tearful confession but a haughty, "The Lord told me to tell you that it is none of your business."

So here we are in 2013 and after living and working and ministering in Germany for almost 13 years, I am still trying to get used to the number of channels on cable television. I was changing the channels one day and I came across Brother Swaggart's televised church service. I have not been keeping up with his life and ministry therefore I had no idea that he was still on television. I watched for a while and believe it or not it felt as if I was experiencing a time warp! Don't get me wrong; the word was being preached, but it seemed as if he and the people were stuck and could not get loose! It was then that questions began to formulate in my mind. I wondered if he had ever been properly restored. I wondered why there seemed to be a "state of stuck in a time warp" for lack of better words. I wondered how God felt about all that had happened and I wondered what we as the body of Christ had learned from all this. Then I thought about, the most recent scandals involving Bishop Eddie Long and the allegations of homosexuality and the sexual abuse of young boys for decades by the priests in the Catholic Church. And the one thing that keeps coming to mind is "Accountability."

To define accountability we must first define what it means to be accountable. Accountable means that we are willingly obligated to report explain or justify something. It means that we willingly answer to somebody. It means that we are willingly subject to someone other than ourselves for what we do and how we do it. But, accountability is not meant for us to control someone's life or allow someone else to control our lives.

We need accountability to keep ourselves from harm and to protect ourselves from harming others. We need to understand that…

- ❖ We are accountable to God first.

    And he was diligent in appointing judges in the land — each of the fortress cities had its judge. He charged the judges: "This is serious work; do it carefully. You are not merely judging between men and women; these are God's judgments that you are passing on. Live in the fear of God—be most careful, for God hates dishonesty, partiality, and bribery" 2 Chronicles 19:6-7 The Message (MSG).

    "Son of man, prophesy against the shepherds, the leaders of Israel. Give them this message from the Sovereign Lord: What sorrow awaits you shepherds who feed yourselves instead of your flocks. Shouldn't shepherds feed their sheep? You drink the milk, wear the wool, and butcher the best animals, but you let your flocks starve. You have not taken care of the weak. You have not tended the sick or bound up the injured. You have not gone looking for those who have wandered away and are lost. Instead, you have ruled them with harshness and cruelty Ezekiel 34:2-4 New Living Translation (NLT).

    "And I tell you this, you must give an account on judgment day for every idle word you speak. The words you say will either acquit you or condemn you" Matthew 12:36-37 New Living Translation (NLT).

    He is especially hard on those who follow their own twisted sexual desire, and who despise authority. These people are proud and arrogant, daring even to scoff at supernatural beings without so much as trembling. But the angels, who are far greater in power and strength, do not dare to bring from the Lord a charge of blasphemy against those supernatural beings 2 Peter 2:10-11 New Living Translation (NLT).

When we accept the fact that we are accountable to God first; we acknowledge our dependency upon him for everything. Pride is an enemy to accountability. It is a force to be reckoned with.

> *So humble yourselves before God. Resist the devil, and he will flee from you. Come close to God, and God will come close to you. Wash your hands, you sinners; purify your hearts, for your loyalty is divided between God and the world. Let there be tears for what you have done. Let there be sorrow and deep grief. Let there be sadness instead of laughter, and gloom instead of joy. Humble yourselves before the Lord, and he will lift you up in honor James 4:7-10 New Living Translation (NLT).*

❖ We are accountable to one another. To allow ourselves to be accountable to someone else, other than God is humbling. The God we serve is a relational God and He created us to be in relationships and to cultivate those relationships. It is fear and pride that will cause us to isolate ourselves.

> *He who willfully separates and estranges himself [from God and man] seeks his own desire and pretext to break out against all wise and sound judgment. Proverbs 18:1-2 Amplified Bible (AMP)*

Humility sets the atmosphere for unity and connectivity.

> *Behold, how good and how pleasant it is for brethren to dwell together in unity! It is like the precious ointment poured on the head, that ran down on the beard, even the beard of Aaron [the first high priest], that came down upon the collar and skirts of his garments [consecrating the whole body]. It is like the dew of [lofty] Mount Hermon and the dew that comes on the hills of Zion; for there the Lord has commanded the blessing, even life forevermore [upon the high and the lowly] Psalm 133 Amplified Bible (AMP).*

When we are accountable to one another it can help us in recognizing what are weaknesses are, you know those areas that we struggle in as we share our lives with one another. We end up challenging each other.

THE MAKING

Just as iron sharpens iron, a person sharpens the character of his friend. Proverbs 27:17 Complete Jewish Bible (CJB)

Where no wise guidance is, the people fall, but in the multitude of counselors there is safety. Proverbs 11:14 Amplified Bible (AMP)

Where there is no counsel, purposes are frustrated, but with many counselors they are accomplished. Proverbs 15:22 Amplified Bible (AMP)

For by wise counsel you can wage your war, and in an abundance of counselors there is victory and safety. Proverbs 24:6 Amplified Bible (AMP) Brethren, if any person is overtaken in misconduct or sin of any sort, you who are spiritual [who are responsive to and controlled by the Spirit] should set him right and restore and reinstate him, without any sense of superiority and with all gentleness, keeping an attentive eye on yourself, lest you should be tempted also. Bear (endure, carry) one another's burdens and troublesome moral faults, and in this way fulfill and observe perfectly the law of Christ (the Messiah) and complete what is lacking [in your obedience to it]. For if any person thinks himself to be somebody [too important to condescend to shoulder another's load] when he is nobody [of superiority except in his own estimation], he deceives and deludes and cheats himself. But let every person carefully scrutinize and examine and test his own conduct and his own work. He can then have the personal satisfaction and joy of doing something commendable [in itself alone] without [resorting to] boastful comparison with his neighbor. For every person will have to bear (be equal to understanding and calmly receive) his own [little] load [of oppressive faults]. Let him who receives instruction in the Word [of God] share all good things with his teacher [contributing to his support]. Do not be deceived and deluded and misled; God will not allow Himself to be sneered at (scorned, disdained, or mocked by mere pretensions or professions, or by His precepts being set aside.) [He inevitably deludes himself who attempts to delude God.] For whatever a man sows, that and that only is what he will reap. For he who sows to his own flesh (lower nature, sensuality) will from the flesh reap decay and ruin and destruction, but he who sows to the Spirit will from the Spirit reap eternal life. And let us not lose heart and grow weary and faint in acting nobly and doing right, for in due time and at the appointed season we shall reap, if we do not loosen and relax our courage and faint. So then, as occasion and opportunity open up to us, let us do good [morally] to all people [not only being useful or profitable to them, but also doing what is for their spiritual good and advantage]. Be mindful to be a blessing, especially to those of the household of faith [those who belong to God's family with you, the believers]. Galatians 6:1-10 Amplified Bible (AMP)

Jim Bakker surrounded himself with "yes men," many of whom had the same weaknesses that he did. Jimmy Swaggart refused to allow himself to be accountable to the elders in the denomination that he was associated with. In both cases there appears to be an absence of humility which, in most cases, is rooted in insensitivity to the Holy Spirit of God who lives in every believer. He is the Convicter and the Convincer. When we stumble and perhaps even fall and fail God so miserably that we think there is no way we can be forgiven, **there is a way to get back up**. A person, who is not convinced that they are sinning, will not repent from the heart of that sin. Where there is no repentance, there is no forgiveness and where there is no forgiveness, there can be no restoration. Jesus lived and died so we could be forgiven and restored to the always intended "right relationship" with God, our Father. When we sin, He is the one who convicts us of the sin. It is up to us whether we respond to his convicting power working in our hearts. True repentance will have a desire to whatever it takes to make things right and want to be changed so that we do not continue to commit the same sin over and repeatedly.

It is our responsibility to live the best lives that we possibly can because we are his representatives to the world. Living lives of accountability is one way that we can do just that. Okay it is examination time.

STUDY QUESTIONS

1. Read 1John 1: 8-10 from at least three translations of the bible. Now write what these passages say about God and what they say about us.

_____
_____
_____
_____
_____
_____

2. Look up the definition for sin, repentance, forgiveness, restoration and restitution and write down below.

_____
_____
_____
_____
_____

3. Now define accountability.

_____
_____
_____
_____
_____

4. Why is there a need for accountability?

5. Who are we to be accountable to first and why?

6. On a very personal level, how does your life reflect that you are being accountable to God?

7. What is one of the greatest enemies to accountability and why?

8. Read Romans 14: 1-23 before answering the following questions. What is the importance of being accountable to one another?

9. Accountability is not to be used as justification for criticism or control but sometimes rebuke and correction may be necessary. How is correction or rebuke to be carried out? Also see Galatians 6: 1-10.

10. How can we be the cause of another believer stumbling and falling?

_____
_____
_____
_____
_____

11. Read Romans 15: 1-4. How does this passage speak to your heart?

_____
_____
_____
_____
_____

12. When we allow ourselves to be accountable to someone else, other than God it is _____.

13. Humility sets the atmosphere for _____ and connectivity.

14. When we are accountable to one another what does it help us to recognize?

_____
_____
_____
_____
_____

15. Who are you are you accountable to in your home? In your church? In your ministry? On your job?

VERA LERAY WARNER

PRACTICUM

Write out a statement of accountability to the Lord.

_____
_____
_____
_____
_____
_____
_____
_____
_____

Write out a statement of accountability to your spouse, your children or someone else to whom you are accountable.

_____
_____
_____
_____
_____
_____
_____
_____

THE MAKING

ALONE WITH THE FATHER

CHAPTER SEVEN

A Minister Ain't Nothing but a Servant (A Review on Servanthood)

For even the Son of Man did not come to be served, but to serve, and to give His life a ransom for man" Mark 10:45 New King James Version.

For even the Son of man came not to be ministered unto, but to minister, and to give his life a ransom for many Mark 10:45 King James Version.

I will start this chapter with a question. Do we, as leaders in ministry, take the use of titles too far? I have personally been called on the carpet more than once for not addressing a female minister as "prophetess so and so." And I have been taken aback when meeting other servants for the first time, and noticing that they made it a point to let me know that they were apostle or prophetess so and so. It was only on very few occasions that Jesus pointedly expressed exactly who He was and then I never read him demanding that they call Him by a specific title. And yet we know that He was and still is the Son of God. I was pondering all of this one day and the thought that came to my mind was, "My given name indicates who I am. The title in front of my name is indicative of what I do." So, when I am called Pastor Vera. I am Vera, daughter of Leroy and Geraldine who is called by God to do the work of a pastor. A pastor is not God, therefore does not deserve the worship, adoration, devotion or loyalty that goes to God and God alone. Rather a pastor is a fellow servant who deserves respect because of the choosing of God for the position. I wonder how many are demanding to be called apostle, prophet, pastor, evangelist, teacher, elder or deacons who have not been specifically chosen by God for the position. Only God knows and we know by the fruit that they bear, and that is not being judgmental! I got so fed up with the misuse and glorification of titles at one point that in this ministry we put minister in front of all the ministry team members names, because a minister, "Ain't nothing but a servant!"

The original Greek word for servant is *diakonos* and it is a verb that means at the least to attend to anything that may serve another's interest. It further means to wait at a table and to offer food and drink to the guests. It means to take care of the poor and sick, i.e. to supply food and the necessities of life (www.the freedictionary.com). I like the idea of a waiter at a table. From the time, you come into the establishment and are shown to your table, that waiter or waitress is there to attend to your every need or desire. And a good waiter will be watchful, coming by your table periodically to refill your glass, replenish your bread and often ask if everything is alright and if you have need of anything. That waiter was hired to be a servant, and is being paid to be a servant and will strive to be the best at what he or she does as the better the service the better the tip. And just think about this; God has given us the Kingdom for our service! Hallelujah!

It was during the 1970s that a man by the name of Robert K. Greenleaf was given credit for the term "Servant Leader." Servant leadership, simply put, is a style of leadership that is expressed through servanthood. The following key points will help us to understand what it means to be a servant leader. I call them the three As of Servant Leadership.

❖ **Attitude:** An attitude of Humility. A servant leader is not master of all, but servant of all. So, then it can be deduced that the first mark of a servant leader is absolute humility. It was the 19th century South African pastor by the name of Andrew Murray who said, "Humility is perfect quietness of heart, it is for me to have no trouble, never to be fretted or vexed or irritated or sore or disappointed. It is to expect nothing, to wonder at nothing done to me, to feel nothing done against me. It is to be at rest when nobody praises me and when I am blamed or despised. It is to have a blessed home in the Lord where I can go in and shut the door and kneel to my Father in secret and be at peace as in a deep sea of calmness when all around is trouble. It is the fruit of the Lord Jesus Christ's redemptive work on Calvary's cross, manifested in those of His own who are definitely subject to the Holy Spirit." A servant leader who walks in humility is subject to the Holy Spirit and therefore will cultivate the heart of a servant rather than expecting to be served by those whom God has placed in their charge. *1 Peter 5: 2-4 says, " Tend (nurture, guard, guide, and fold) the flock of God that is [your responsibility], not by coercion or constraint, but willingly; not dishonorably motivated by the advantages and profits [belonging to the office], but eagerly and cheerfully Not domineering [as arrogant, dictatorial, and overbearing persons] over those in your charge, but being examples (patterns and models of Christian living) to the flock (the congregation). And [then] when the Chief Shepherd is revealed, you will win the conqueror's crown of* *glory."* From this passage of scripture, we get the idea of the protection and nurturing of those whom God has placed in our care. Servant leadership is not about power and control. The leader who is geared toward power and concerned for his or her own needs more that the growth and needs of those placed in their charge may be prone to cynicism (mis-trust), perfectionism, and jockeying for position. This goes right back to the lead scripture for this chapter. Jesus and the disciples were on their way to Jerusalem and he began to tell them what he would suffer leading up to the crucifixion and resurrection. James and John went to him and asked for a favor, to sit in a place of honor, power, influence, and authority when he came into his Kingdom. Their request, when the others heard of it, created an atmosphere of anger and contention. And of course, the Master of All steps in and begins to explain to them what it means to be a true servant in the Kingdom of God. He summed it all up, in that He himself came to serve and not to be served. A minister Ain't nothing but a servant.

❖ **Availability:** The servant leader must live a life that says, "I am here for you, even if it is not convenient for me, because I care and I respect you. I recognize your value and I have your best interest in mind." This will mean having such a close-knit relationship with the Lord that we become skilled at prioritizing. *Greater love hath no man than this that a man lays down his life for his friends (John 15:13 KJV).* I remember the story about a woman who was right in the midst of hot and heavy prayer and she kept feeling prompted to call a particular friend and the more she prayed the stronger the nudging and she said to the Lord, "Lord, don't you see me praying, isn't this more important than seeing about my friend." And the Lord spoke to her that obedience was better than sacrifice. Yes, being in the presence of the Lord is the most important thing, but we also have to do as well. Lord, help us to be so sensitive to your Spirit, to follow your leading and not our own! Help us to be available at a moment's notice even if it is in convenient.

❖ **Advancement:** The servant leader is to always build up and help bring out the best in the people that they are leading. I call this, "Up and Out." It is building them up and allowing God to use us to help bring out the very best in them! It is the concept of empowering them and then releasing them to be all and do all God has purposed. We have all heard the expression, "He brings out the best in me." Well, have you ever been around someone and your interaction with them always seems to bring out the worst in you? Chances are you do everything you can not to be around that person. In fact, when you see them coming, you go the other way. I am convinced that God intends for us to be the type of leaders who it is a joy to be around because we always tend to bring out the best of what they are inside. We serve a progressive God and this means that He is always, progressively, working on us. And I am convinced and sure of this very thing, that *He Who began a good work in you will continue until the day of Jesus Christ [right up to the time of His* *return], developing [that good work] and perfecting and bringing it to full completion in you (Philippians 1:6 Amplified Bible).* We empower them by teaching them who they are in Christ and how God can and will use them to make a difference. And then releasing them, and not hindering their growth by holding them back to help further our own ministries. A minister Ain't nothing but a servant!

To truly be a minister in the Kingdom of God is to first and foremost have an attitude of complete humility. This attitude of humility is an ongoing work of the Holy Spirit in our lives. Because just as soon as we feel that we have reached some stage of humility in our lives, it is God who shows us, usually through circumstances just how prideful we really are. We must come to the realization that we are master of none and God is Master of All! We can do nothing of worth, apart from God and our dependency must, be upon him for everything. We must carefully, methodically, examine the way Jesus lead and follow his example. It sounds impossible, doesn't it? However, God will never ask us to do that which He will not equip us for. He builds us up with himself and brings out the very best in us at the best possible time! Whatever leaders choose to be called or addressed; titles come and titles go but it is a saved, sanctified life that will stand forever! And a minister Ain't nothing but a servant!

STUDY QUESTIONS

1. Read Mark 10: 17-45 from at least three translations of the Bible. In verses 17-31. List some things that Jesus said concerning eternal life.

_____
_____
_____
_____
_____

2. A leader can be described as someone out in front who assists, supervises, or directs another individual or group of individuals in certain matters concerning life. Now write down the definition of a servant then write down a definition for servant-leader.

_____
_____
_____
_____
_____

3. What does being a servant-leader have to do with eternal life?

_____
_____
_____
_____

4. What are the three As of Servant-Leadership?

5. The first mark of a servant leader is humility. Write in your own words a good definition of humility.

6. Read 1 Peter 5: 2-4. Explain how this passage conveys the idea of protecting and nurturing those whom God has placed in our care.

7. What problems might the servant leader who is geared toward power and control face?

8. What does it mean to you to lead by example?

9. List some ways that Jesus led by example and provide the scripture reference for each example.

10. Read the following passages of scripture and describe servanthood in each passage…i.e. the nation, the Messiah. Isaiah 42:1-4; 49: 1-6; 50:4-9; 52: 13-53:12.

_____
_____
_____
_____
_____

11. Now read Ephesians 4: 11-13 and 1 Peter 4: 8-11. Explain your understanding of each passage in regard to servant-leadership.

_____
_____
_____
_____
_____

12. What is the best way that a servant-leader can cultivate a life style of availability?

_____
_____
_____
_____
_____
_____

13. Explain the "Up and Out" concept in being a servant-leader.

14. How important is the commitment of the servant-leader to those whom they are leading and why?

15. Look up the word progressive in the dictionary. Now, what do we mean if we say that we serve a progressive God?

16. How do we empower those whom we lead and what does it mean to release them?

17. What does to not release them say about the servant-leader and what type of implications can this have?

PRACTICUM

Write out an honest statement of your personal attitude concerning leadership in the Kingdom of God.

_____
_____
_____
_____
_____
_____
_____

Write a letter to a leader in your personal life, whether past or present, dead or alive that had a major positive impact upon your life, thanking them for their labor of love and obedience in the Kingdom.

If you are a servant in a leadership position; ask yourself the following questions and write down honest answers…

❖ Is progressive spiritual health evident in those whom I am leading and if not, what is the reason?

_____
_____
_____
_____
_____
_____
_____

❖ Is spiritual freedom evident in those whom I am leading and if not, what is the reason for their lack of spiritual freedom?

VERA LERAY WARNER

ALONE WITH THE FATHER

BIBLIOGRAPHY

Heartlights Search God's Word, The New Testament Greek Lexicon (http://www.searchgodsword.org).

MacDonald, William. *Believer's Bible Commentary* (Nashville, TN, Nelson Publishers, 1995).

Study Light (http://www.studylight.com).

The Free Dictionary (http://www.thefreedictionary.com).

ABOUT THE AUTHOR

Vera LeRay Warner is founder and President of In His Image: Women of Excellence Ministries. It is a ministry founded upon biblical principles whose vision is to see women saved and set free by the grace of God and sent forth, empowered by the Holy Spirit, to make an impact upon the world. Their annual European conference has attendees from all over the world. Their annual and biennial USA conferences are testaments of God's favor and love and power! And through their G.A.L.s (God's Apple Ladies) Bible Study groups lives are being changed forever!

Vera is a graduate of Wayland Baptist University where she earned a Bachelor's degree in Christian Education and in 2006 she earned her a Master's degree in Theology. She is an author, and her published works include, <u>Creatively Reaping the Harvest, Embracing the Love of the Father, Speak to Me Lord, Inspirational Writings by Women for Women, and Cultivate My Heart</u>. Vera is first and foremost a Bible Teacher, who flows under a prophetic anointing. She continues to travel in the United States and abroad ministering at retreats, seminars, revivals and banquets.

In the past she has served in numerous positions in the local church as well as the military chapel to include, but was not limited to: Sunday School Teacher, Children's Church Leader, Intercessory Prayer Group Leader, Women's Ministries President, Church Administrator, PWOC Chapter President, Praise and Worship Team member, and Adult Bible Study Teacher.

Vera honorably served in the United States Air Force for almost 12 years and during that, time was selected and listed in the 1984 edition of, "Outstanding Young Women in America."

She is married to Michael Warner, Sr. who is a retired United States Army Warrant Officer. Together, they have pastored churches in Germany for eleven years. They are the parents of two grown children and have seven grandchildren. The Warners currently reside in Columbia, SC.

CONNECT WITH AUTHOR VERA LERAY WARNER

Friend me on Facebook: https://www.facebook.com/embracingHislove/

Twitter: https://twitter.com/veraleray

Subscribe to my blog: http://www.veraleraywarner.com/veras-blog/index.html

Visit my website: http://www.veraleraywarner.com/

He is the core of my being!

Embracing the Love of the Father is a call to people everywhere, but especially to those who, for whatever reason, have not allowed themselves to be truly loved by the Father. This book is a reminder that He loves us so much and desires that we not just recognize His love for us but that we accept it as truth and embrace it with everything within us. This book re-emphasizes that we are "spiritual Israel". Therefore, we are the "apple of His eye", but most importantly, He is the "core" of our being.

"*Embracing the Love of the Father*" gives the very important foundation about the true Love of God in our searching we allow Him to establish a unique and everlasting personal love relationship. While studying the book and the scriptures, as well as working on your personal answers and inviting God to speak to you; God will guide you to a new level of faith and freedom (John 8:32) by revealing to you His truth and His Love.

Dr. Andreas and Gabriele Haun
Mühltal, Germany

I have read this book and studied from it as well. It is a great tool to uncover those problem areas that you may not even be aware of that need to be uncovered. *Embracing the Love of the Father* is so freeing and so personal that you cannot help but view yourself and how the Father loves you.

This book will prove to be an invaluable investment into your life. Your life will be truly changed.

Andrea Johnson, United Kingdom

I Need a Heart fix!

The title of this study starts off with the word "cultivate" as does each of the chapter titles. "Cultivate" is a word used a lot in farming or agriculture and it means to prepare the land or the ground for use. It means to loosen or break up the soil. It further means to improve by labor, care or study. The heart is that ground that initially needs to be prepared by God to receive the seed of His Word.

Cultivate my Heart is a great resource that gives way for great discussion to take place if within a group setting and also deep reflection!

Samantha Roach United Kingdom

Glad I did this study after "Embracing the Love of the Father", because when He started cultivating I needed to remind myself that He was doing it in love. It is more like open-heart surgery; only you are fully awake. If you feel you need to go deeper with the Lord and bring forth much lasting fruit, then I strongly recommend this book.

Joyce Luutu, Author
United Kingdom

Made in the USA
Columbia, SC
14 March 2024